HAIR!
THE MUSICAL

WISE PUBLICATIONS
part of The Music Sales Group

London / New York / Paris / Sydney / Copenhagen / Berlin / Madrid / Hong Kong / Tokyo

Published by
Wise Publications
14-15 Berners Street, London W1T 3LJ, UK.

Exclusive Distributors:
Music Sales Limited
Distribution Centre, Newmarket Road,
Bury St Edmunds, Suffolk IP33 3YB, UK.
Music Sales Corporation
180 Madison Avenue, 24th Floor, New York NY 10016, USA.
Music Sales Pty Limited
4th floor, Lisgar House, 30-32 Carrington Street,
Sydney, NSW 2000, Australia.

Order No. AM1010493
ISBN: 978-1-78305-943-0
This book © Copyright 2015 Wise Publications,
a division of Music Sales Limited.

Compiled and edited by Jenni Norey.
Music arranged by Alistair Watson.
Music processed by Paul Ewers Music Design.
Cover design by Tim Field.
Cover photograph of Marsha Hunt by
Mike McKeown/Daily Express/Hulton Archive/Getty Images.
Cover image from Fotolia.com

Printed in the EU.

INTRO

The continuing appeal of *Hair: The American Tribal Love-Rock Musical* might have come as a surprise to those who fell in love with it during its off-Broadway six-week premiere run back in 1967. *Hair's* exuberant rejoicing in the hippie counterculture and its loose construction made it more of a current happening than a traditional stage musical. The brainchild of two actors, Gerome Ragni and James Rado (who wrote the book and lyrics), *Hair* seems to have lasted not despite, but perhaps because of its rejection of conventional structure. The Sixties were all about the spontaneous excitement of the streets which, as James Rado later suggested, "was very important historically, and if we hadn't written *Hair*, there'd not be any examples. You could read about it and see film clips, but you'd never experience it".

That initial short run gradually expanded into other venues, other cities and eventually all over the world. Galt MacDermot wrote the music for Ragni and Rado's passionate synthesis of their volatile friendship, recasting themselves as Berger (the extrovert one) and Claude (the contemplative one), leaders of the counterculture 'Tribe'. There have been many structural reworkings of *Hair*, as befits such an organic enterprise, but the songs and narrative have stayed more or less the same.

'Aquarius' was the show opener, an anthem heralding a new age of brotherly love. 'Donna' is an impressionistic song about a spiritual and carnal quest to find 'a sixteen year old virgin' (remember, this was the Sixties…) while 'Manchester, England' is a claim by a native New Yorker to have come from the British city, reminding us that *Hair* dates from a decade when the UK was seen as a youth culture trend setter. 'Ain't Got No' is an ironic list of rejected materialism and matching beliefs: ain't got no home, no shoes, no money, no class, no God…

'Air' is an early satirical swipe at urban pollution and 'I Got Life' is a tribe leader's anti-materialistic riposte to parental accusations that he doesn't own anything. Ingenue Crissy sings 'Frank Mills', a plea to a boy she met once and wants to see again even though their first and only encounter left her two dollars poorer. 'Hair' is a musical justification of the show's title, a celebration of nature unfettered, after which — in a rare moment of self-doubt — a tribe member sings 'Where Do I Go?'. Act I ends with the once-racy scene where the entire tribe emerges on stage naked, chanting words of peace and harmony.

Act 2 starts with 'Black Boys/White Boys', where white girls celebrate the appeal of black boys and black girls admire 'pretty' white boys. 'Easy To Be Hard' reflects a serio-comic montage of conflicts, killings and persecutions that takes *Hair* into its darkest sequence, to be alleviated by the sweetly melodic and hopeful 'Good Morning Starshine'. Even so the show's original ending remained downbeat, finishing with 'The Flesh Failures', a catalogue of gloom prompted by the death of Claude, a leader of the tribe who had in the end been reluctantly conscripted into the military. In a bid to lighten the closing moments, 'Let The Sunshine In' was added to provide a joyous and hopeful conclusion to a great 60s musical experience that still shows few signs of aging despite being forever fixed in its own psychedelic timeframe. Instead of looking dated, *Hair* can even seem touching as new productions mounted in more cynical times continue to revisit this uplifting and hope-filled Sixties subversion of the traditional Broadway musical.

AQUARIUS

Words by James Rado & Gerome Ragni
Music by Galt MacDermot

love_____ will steer the stars. This is the dawn-ing of the

age of A-qua-ri-us,___ the age of A-qua-ri-us,___

A-qua-ri-us!___ A-

-qua-ri-us!___

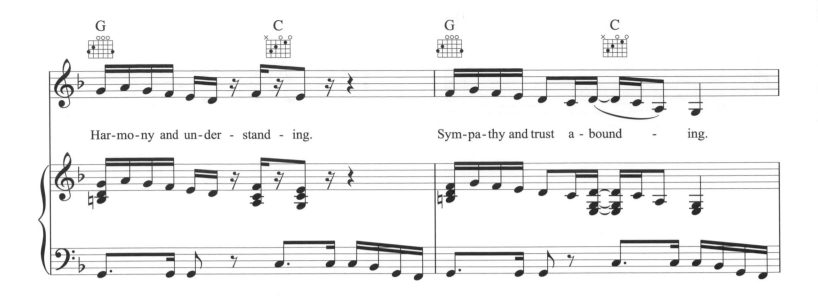

Har-mo-ny and un-der - stand - ing. Sym-pa-thy and trust a - bound - ing.

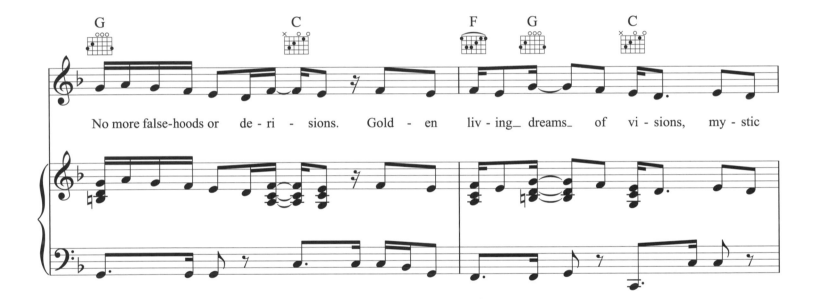

No more false-hoods or de - ri - sions. Gold - en liv - ing___ dreams___ of vi - sions, my - stic

cry - stal re - ve - la - tion and the mind's___ true li - be - ra - tion.___ A -

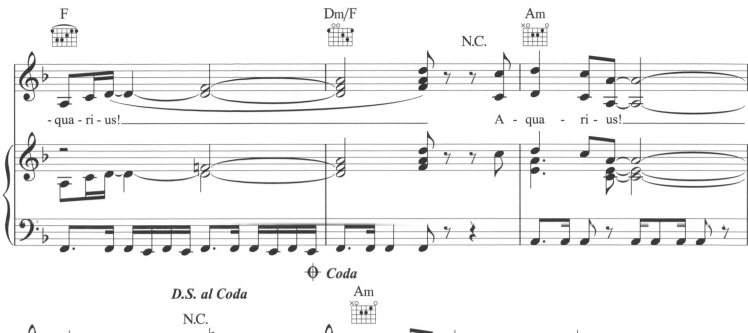

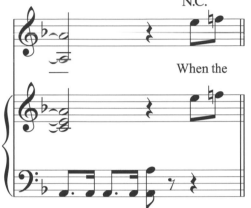

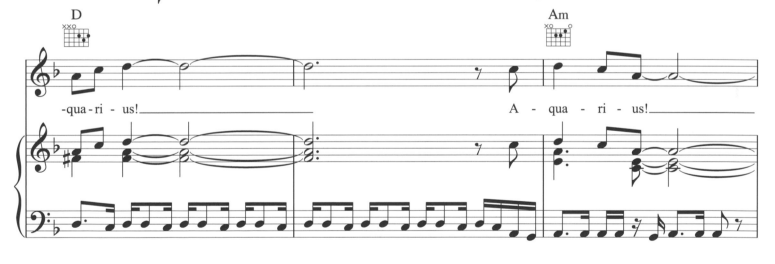

DONNA

Words by James Rado & Gerome Ragni
Music by Galt MacDermot

Once up-on a look-ing for Don - na - time_ there was a six - teen year old vir - gin.

Oh, Don - na, oh oh, Don - na, oh oh oh, look - ing for_ my Don - na._

Just got back from look-ing for Don - na, San___ Fran-cis-co, psy-che - de - lic ur - chin.

Oh, Don-na, oh oh, Don-na, oh oh oh, look-ing for___ my Don - na.___

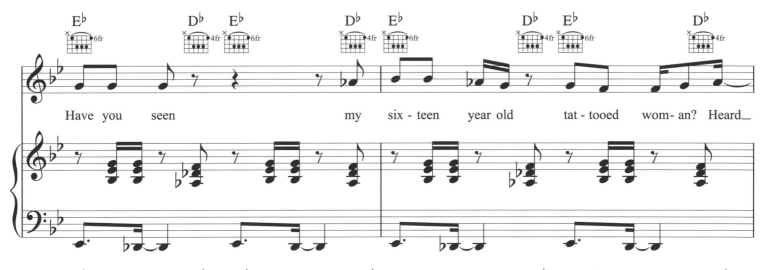

Have you seen my six - teen year old tat - tooed wom- an? Heard___

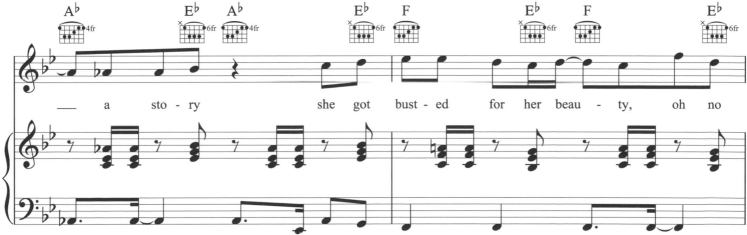

___ a sto - ry she got bust - ed for her beau - ty, oh no

9

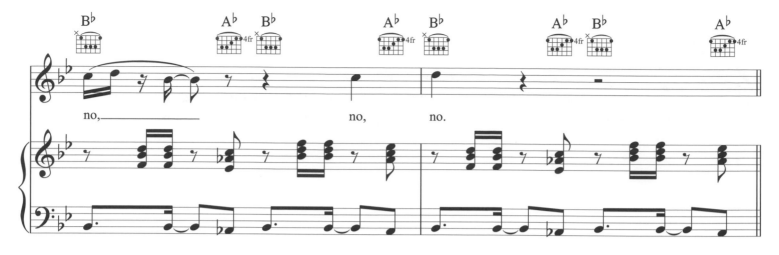

Once up-on a look-ing for Don - na, San_ Fran-cis-co, nev - er end my search - ing.

Oh, Don-na, oh oh, Don-na, oh oh oh, look-ing for__ my Don - na.__

I've been__ to In - di - a and saw the yo - gi light.
And I'm gon - na__ show her__ life on earth__ can be sweet.

10

down. (That you put down.)

Once up-on a look-ing for Don-na - time_ there was a six-teen year old vir-gin.

Oh, Don-na, oh oh, Don-na, oh oh oh, look-ing for_ my Don-na._

Look-ing for_ my Don-na,_ look-ing for_ my Don-na._ Don-na!

MANCHESTER, ENGLAND

Words by James Rado & Gerome Ragni
Music by Galt MacDermot

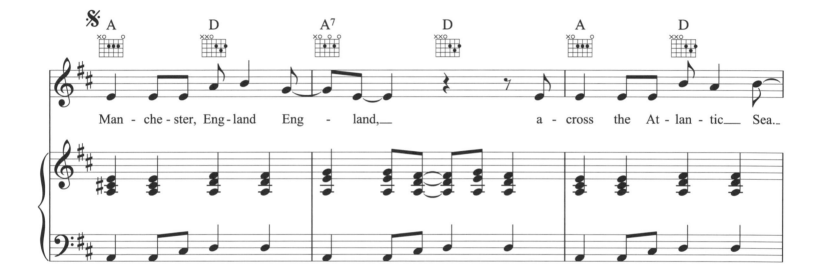

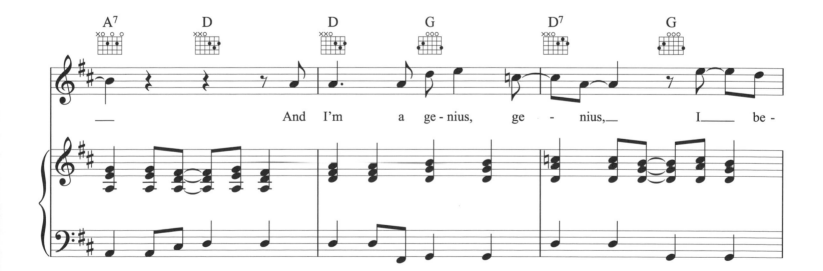

Hoop-er Bu-kows-ki._ Now that I've dropped_ out

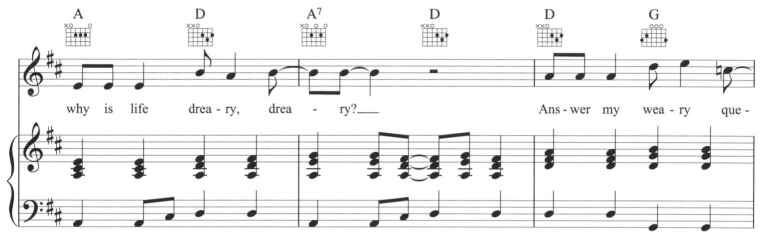

why is life drea-ry, drea-ry?_ Ans-wer my wea-ry que-

-ry._ Whoa,_ Tim-o-thy Lea-ry,_ dea-rie._ Oh,

me. Ah, that's me. Ah, that's me. Ah ha ha.
(That's he.) (That's he.) (That's he.)

D.S. al Coda

𝄌 *Coda*

15

I'M BLACK/AIN'T GOT NO

Words by James Rado & Gerome Ragni
Music by Galt MacDermot

home,   ain't got no shoes,   ain't got no mon-ey,   ain't got no
(2.) moth - er,   ain't got no cul - ture,   ain't got no friends,   ain't got no
(3.) smokes,   ain't got no job,   ain't got no work,   ain't got no

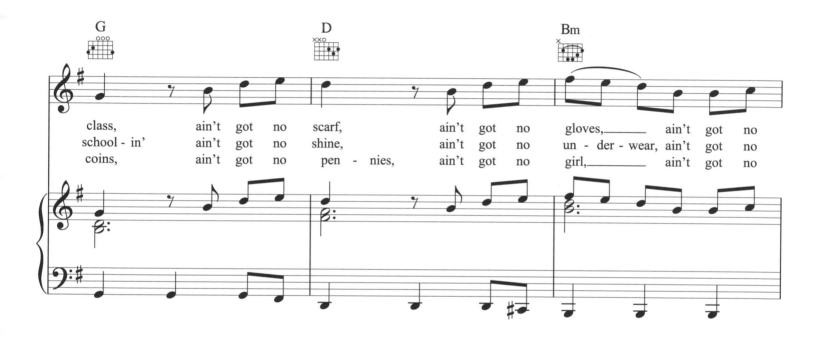

class,   ain't got no scarf,   ain't got no gloves,   ain't got no
school - in'   ain't got no shine,   ain't got no un - der - wear, ain't got no
coins,   ain't got no pen - nies,   ain't got no girl,   ain't got no

Play 3 times

bed,   ain't got no pot,   ain't got no faith.   2. Ain't got no
soap,   ain't got no A - Train,   ain't got no mind.   3. Ain't got no
tick-et,   ain't got no to - ken,   ain't got no God.   Ain't got no

trees, ain't got no air, ain't got no wa- ter, cit- y, ban- jo, tooth-picks, shoe-lace, tea- chers, foot- ball, te- le- phone,

re-cords, doc-tor, broth-er, sis- ter, u- ni-forms, ma-chine guns, air-planes, germs, M - 1; bang__ bang bang. M-

-2; bang__ bang bang. A bombs, H bombs, P bombs, Q bombs, Chi-nese checks, Hin-dus, Bin-dus, I-

-ta-li-a-nos, Pol-lacks, Ger-mans, Yous, Jews, ups and downs. Vi-et-nam, John-son, high school, sex, cof-fee,

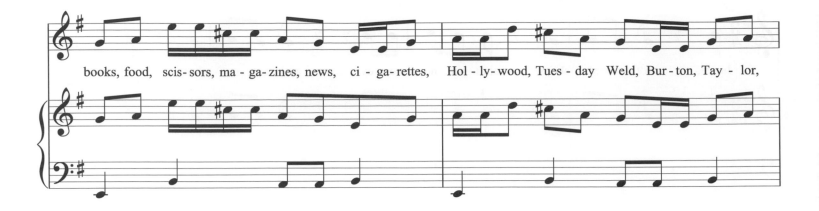

books, food, scis-sors, ma-ga-zines, news, ci-ga-rettes, Hol-ly-wood, Tues-day Weld, Bur-ton, Tay-lor,

pop art, pop off, pop-corn, pop-si-cle, An-dy War-pop, pop pa-per, pop

Pop-eye, pop-pers, En-gland, ou-ter space, a-stro-nauts, Je-sus, air, air, air, air,

G/A

B

air, air, air!_____ Ain't got no

AIR

Words by James Rado & Gerome Ragni
Music by Galt MacDermot

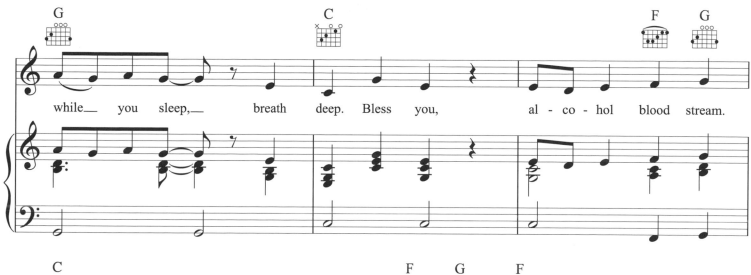

while_ you sleep,_ breath deep. Bless you, al - co - hol blood stream.

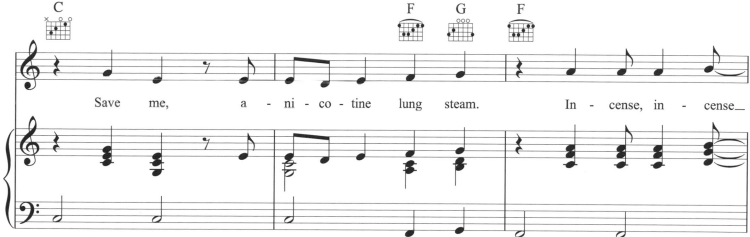

Save me, a - ni - co - tine lung steam. In - cense, in - cense_

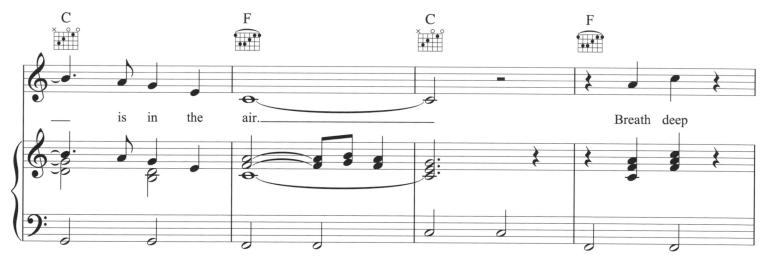

_ is in the air._____ Breath deep

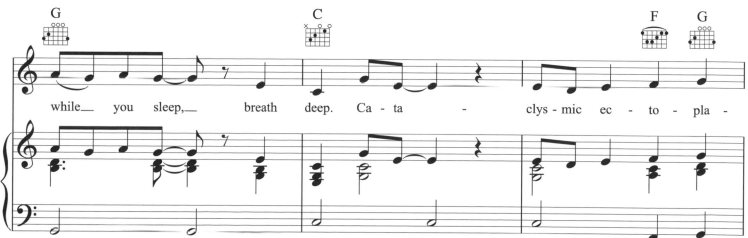

while_ you sleep,_ breath deep. Ca - ta - clys - mic ec - to - pla -

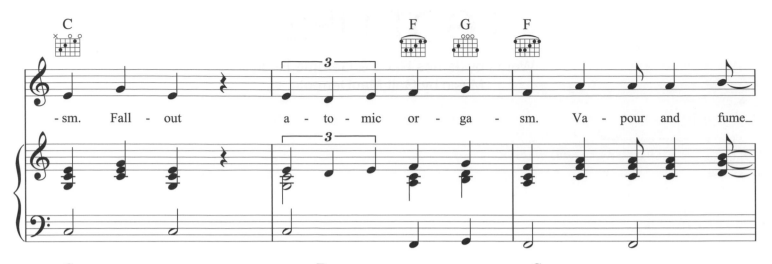

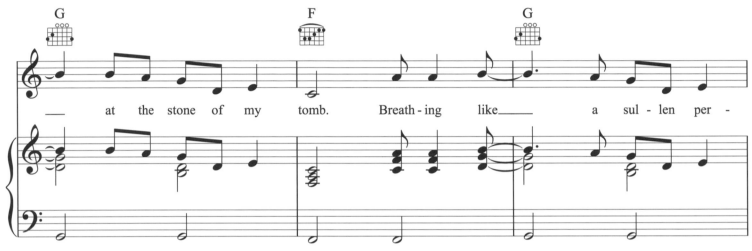

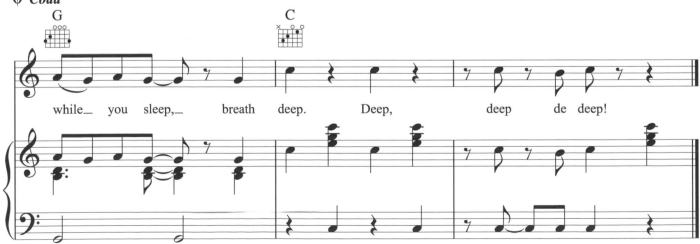

I GOT LIFE

Words by James Rado & Gerome Ragni
Music by Galt MacDermot

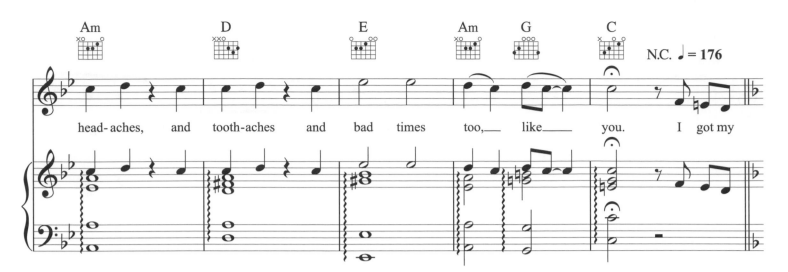

head-aches, and tooth-aches and bad times too,___ like___ you. I got my

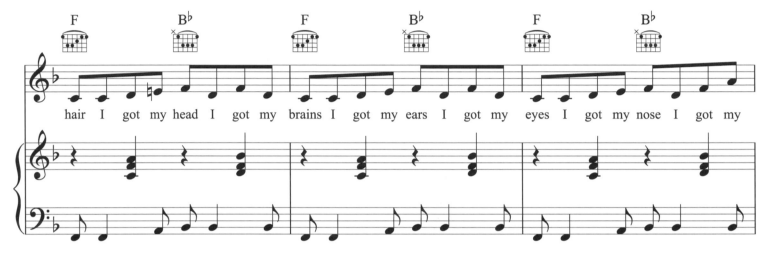

hair I got my head I got my brains I got my ears I got my eyes I got my nose I got my

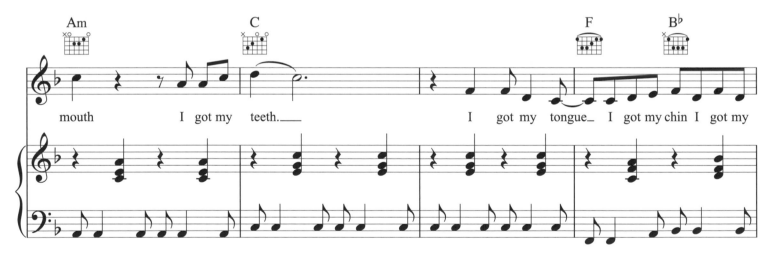

mouth I got my teeth.___ I got my tongue_ I got my chin I got my

neck I got my tits I got my heart I got my soul I got my back I got my

ass._____   I got my arms_____ I got my hands I got my

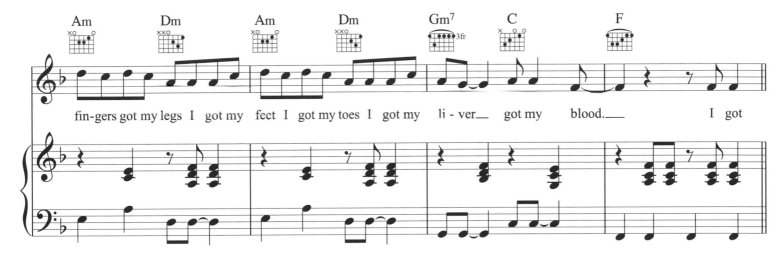

fin-gers got my legs I got my feet I got my toes I got my li-ver___ got my blood.___   I got

life,   moth - er,___   I got laughs,   sis - ter.___   I got

free - dom,_   broth-er,___   I got good good times,_   good times, man._ I got

cra-zy ways, daugh-ter, I got a mil-lion-dol-lar charm, cou-sin.___ I got

head-aches and tooth-aches and bad times too,___ like you._____ I got my hair_

___ I got my hands I got my brains I got my ears I got my eyes I got my nose I got my mouth got___ my

teeth._____ I got my tongue_ I got my chin I got my neck I got my tits I got my

28

FRANK MILLS

Words by James Rado & Gerome Ragni
Music by Galt MacDermot

31

He lives in Brook - lyn_ some - where and

wears this white crash hel - met. He has gold chains on his

lea - ther jack - et___ and on the back are writ - ten the names_

'Mar - y' and 'Mom' and_ 'Hell's_ An - gels'.___

HAIR

Words by James Rado & Gerome Ragni
Music by Galt MacDermot

twist-ed, bead-ed, braid-ed, pow-ered, flow-ered and___ con-fet-tied,_ ban-

-gled, tan-gled, span-gled and spa-ghet-tied._____ Oh

say, can you see my_____ eyes? If you

can then my hair's too short. Down to here, down to there, down to there, down to where it

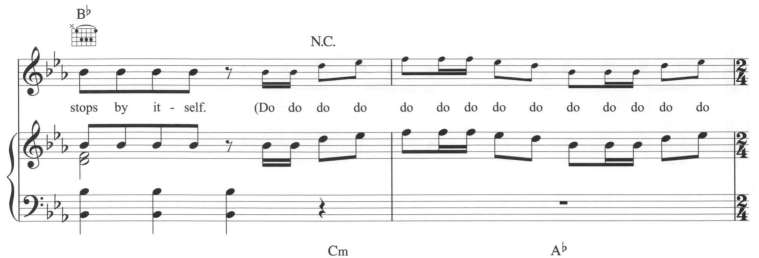

stops by it -self. (Do do do do do do do do do do do do do do

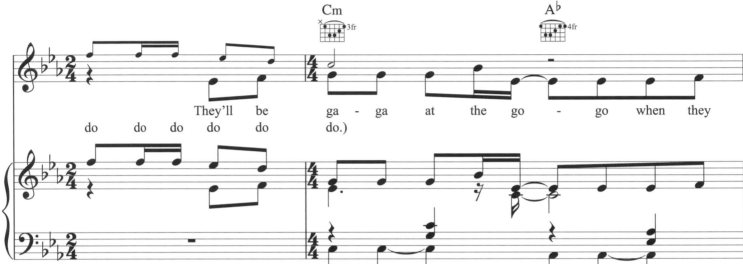

do do do do do do.) They'll be ga - ga at the go - go when they

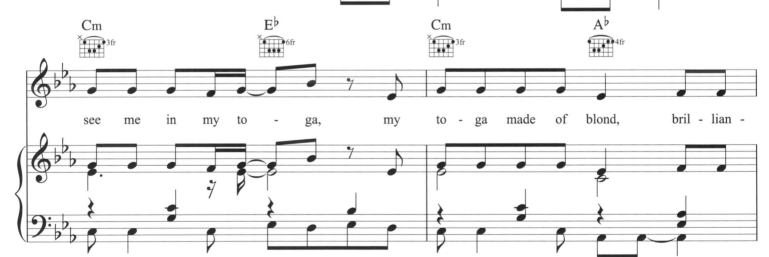

see me in my to - ga, my to - ga made of blond, bril - lian -

-tined, bi - bli - cal hair. My hair like Je - sus wore__ it, Hal - le - lu -

WHERE DO I GO?

Words by James Rado & Gerome Ragni
Music by Galt MacDermot

42

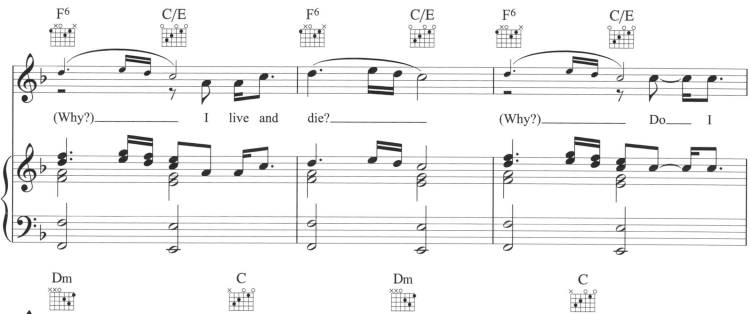

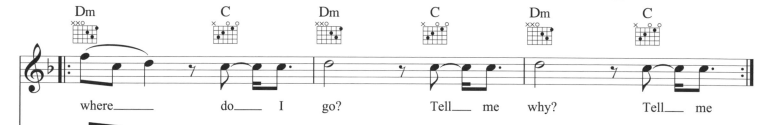

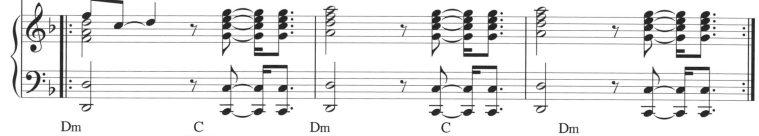

BLACK BOYS/WHITE BOYS

Words by James Rado & Gerome Ragni
Music by Galt MacDermot

1. Black boys are de-li-cious, choc-'late fla-voured love.__
2. Black boys are nu-tri-cious, black boys fill me up.__

Li-c'rice lips like can-dy, keep my co-coa hand-y.
Black boys are so damn yum-my, they sa-tis-fy__ my tum-my.

46

And when my dad-dy tells me "Stay a - way"_____ I just say, "Come on out an'

play - ay". Yeah yeah yeah, white boys_____ are so_____ groo - vy.

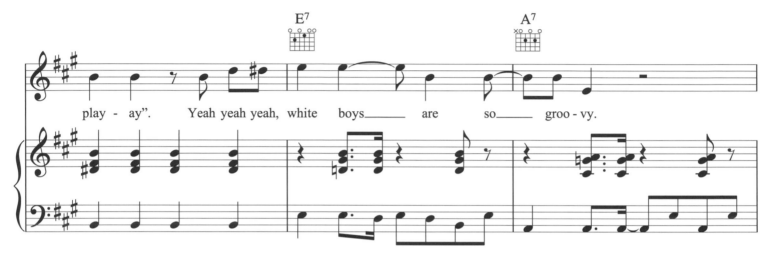

White boys are so tough._____ And ev - 'ry time that they're near_

_____ me I just can't get e - nough._____

1. White boys____ are   so____ pret - ty,____   white boys   are so   sweet.__
2. White boys____ are   so____ sex - y,____   legs   so   long an'   lean.__
% White boys____ are   so____ love - ly,____   beau - ti - ful as   girls.__

____   White boys   drive me   cra - zy,
____   I   love   those   sprayed - on   trou - sers,
____   I love to run my____   fin - gers

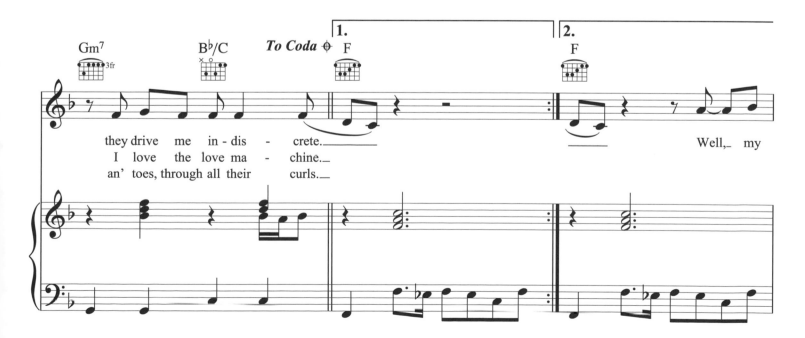

they drive me in - dis - crete.____   ____   Well,_ my
I love   the love ma - chine.__
an' toes, through all their curls.__

broth - er calls 'em rub - ble_____

but they're my_____ kind of trou - ble._____

That's why my dad - dy tells me "No, no, no,_____ no"_____

D.S. al Coda   ⊕ ***Coda***

I just say, "White boys go,_____ go go,_____ go, go, go".

Give me a

soft, a sweet, a sex-y, a love-ly a jui-cy de-li-cious:

White boy! Black boy! White boy!

Black boy! White boy! Mixed me-di-a!

Play 3 times

51

EASY TO BE HARD

Words by James Rado & Gerome Ragni
Music by Galt MacDermot

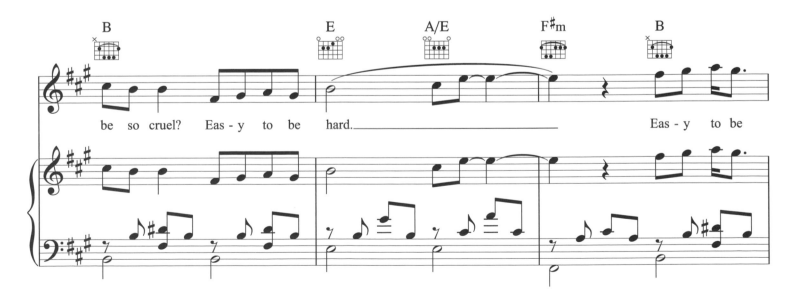

GOOD MORNING STARSHINE

Words by James Rado & Gerome Ragni
Music by Galt MacDermot

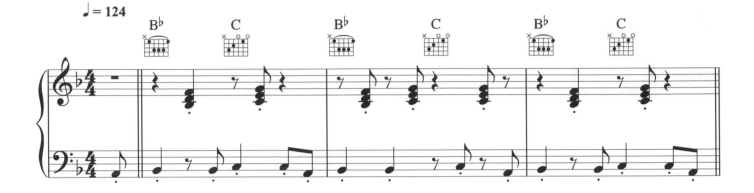

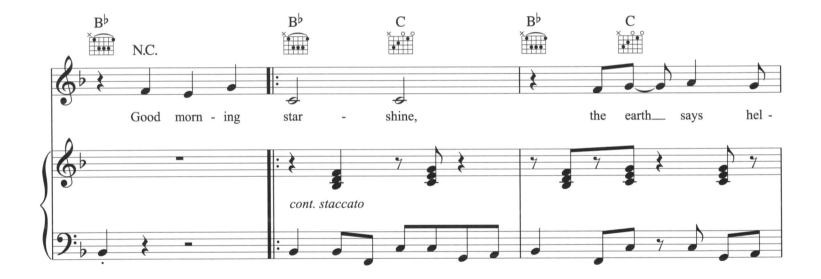

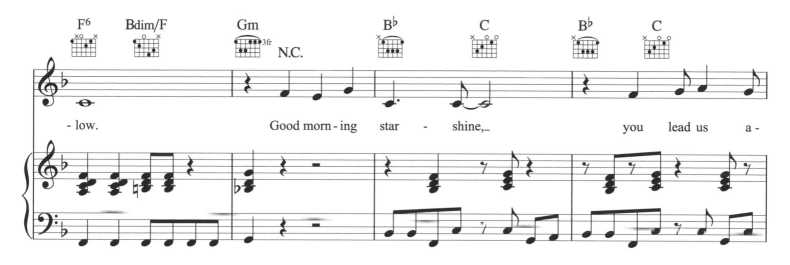

-low. Good morn-ing star - shine,___ you lead us a-

-long; my love and me___ as___ we sing___

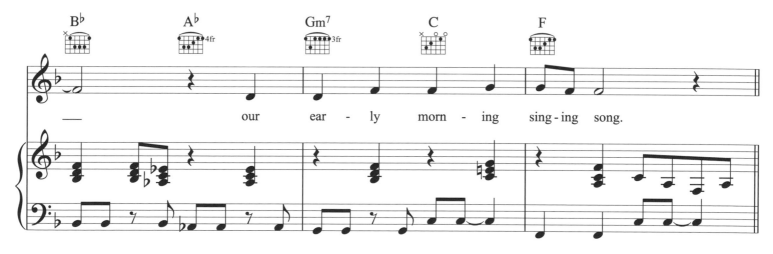

___ our ear - ly morn - ing sing-ing song.

Glid - dy glub gloo - py nib - by nab - by noo - py, la la la, lo lo.___

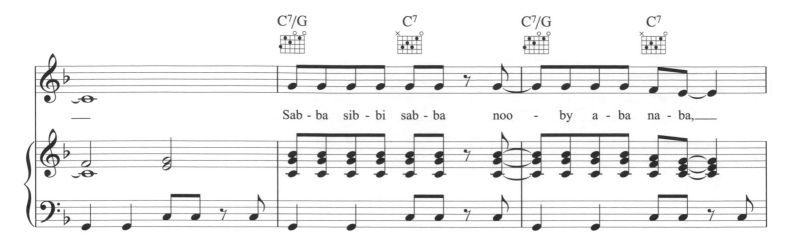

Sab - ba sib - bi sab - ba noo - by a - ba na - ba,___

lee lee, lo lo._____ Too - by oo - by wa - la noo-

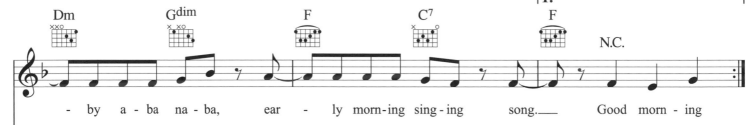

- by a - ba na - ba, ear - ly morn-ing sing-ing song.___ Good morn - ing

Sing - in' a song,___ hum-min' a song,_____

sing - in' a song. _____ Lov - in' a song,___

laugh-in' a song,_____ sing - ing a song._____

Sing the song,___ song the sing.___ Song, song, song sing,_____

___ sing, sing, sing song._____

THE FLESH FAILURES/
LET THE SUNSHINE IN

Words by James Rado & Gerome Ragni
Music by Galt MacDermot

Man - ches - ter, Eng - land Eng - land a - cross the At - lan - tic Sea.

And I'm a ge - nius, ge - nius,__ I__ be - lieve in__ God__

and I be - lieve that__ God be - lieves in__ Claude, that's me. That's

me, that's__ me.__

D.S. al Coda

Sing - ing our space songs on a spi-der web si - tar.___

Life is a - round___ you and in_____ you. Ans-wer for Tim - o - thy Lea - ry, dea -

- rie.___ Let the sun - shine,_____

let the sun - shine in,___ the sun - shine in.

Repeat to fade

123456789